DC SUPER HEROES

KNOCK-KNOCK JOKES

BY MICHAEL DAHL
& DONALD LEMKE

STONE ARCH BOOKS
a capstone imprint

Published by Capstone Young Readers in 2018
A Capstone Imprint
1710 Roe Crest Drive
North Mankato, Minnesota 56003
www.capstonepub.com

STAR39969

Cataloging-in-Publication Data is available on the
Library of Congress website.

ISBN: 978-1-4965-5764-3 (library hardcover)
ISBN: 978-1-4965-5768-1 (eBook)

Summary: Knock knock! Who's there? Robin. Robin who? Robbing is for
criminals — not super heroes! With KNOCK-KNOCK jokes featuring
Batman, Superman, and Wonder Woman, this official DC Comics joke
book will have readers coming back for more!

Designer: Brann Garvey

Printed in China.
010734S18

HA!
HA!
HA!

DC SUPER HEROES
KNOCK-KNOCK
JOKES

HA!
HA!
HA!

HA!
HA!
HA!

HA!
HA!
HA!

Knock, knock!
Who's there?
Jet
Jet who?
Jet the back door, it's cold outside!

Knock, knock!
Who's there?
Wonder
Wonder who?
Wonder come out and play?

Knock, knock!
Who's there?
Diana.
Diana who?
Diana meet you! I'm your biggest fan!

Knock, knock!
Who's there?
Anita
Anita who?
Anita super hero to come help me!

Knock, knock!
Who's there?
Kanga!
Kanga who?
No, Kangaroo!

Knock, knock!
Who's there?
Perry
Perry who?
Perry-dice Island is where Wonder Woman comes from!

SUPERMAN!

Knock, knock!
Who's there?

Krypton
Krypton who?

Krypton side Superman's Fortress without being caught!

Knock, knock!
Who's there?
Mikey
Mikey who?
Mikey won't open the Fortress of Solitude?

Knock, knock!
Who's there?
Luke
Luke who?
Luke out! Here comes Superman!

Knock, knock!
Who's there?
Amos
Amos who?
Amos Supergirl fan!

Knock, knock!
Who's there?
Jimmy.
Jimmy who?
Jimmy some food. I'm starving!

Knock, knock!
Who's there?
Clark Kent.
Clark Kent who?
**Clark Kent come over to play
today, he's sick!**

Knock, knock!
Who's there?
Olive?
Olive who?
**Olive you, Superman!
(It's me, Lois.)**

Knock, knock!
Who's there?
Donut
Donut who?

Donut ask, it's Bizarro!

Knock, knock!
Who's there?
Super.
Super who?
Soup or salad!

Knock, knock!
Who's there?
Lex.
Lex who?
Lex like my tooth is really looth!

Knock, knock!
Who's there?
Canoe!
Canoe who?
Canoe help us, Superman?

Knock, knock!

Who's there?

Iowa.

Iowa who?

Iowa lot to Superman for rescuing me!

Knock, knock!

Who's there?

Ivana

Ivana who?

Ivana fly like Superman!

Knock, knock!
Who's there?
Olsen?
Olsen who?
Olsen another sweep if you won't let the first one in!

Knock, knock!
Who's there?
Lois Lane
Lois Lane who?
Lois Lane down right now; she's tired from her adventure!

Knock, knock!
Who's there?
Luthor.
Luthor who?
Luthor than it was yesterday!

Knock, knock!
Who's there?
Cape.
Cape who?
**Cape put away your homework
and come outside, okay?**

Knock, knock!
Who's there?
Mister Wayne.
Mister Wayne who?
**Mister Wayne last night, cuz
everything's wet out here!**

Knock, knock!
Who's there?
Athena
Athena who?
Athena Bat-Signal in the sky!

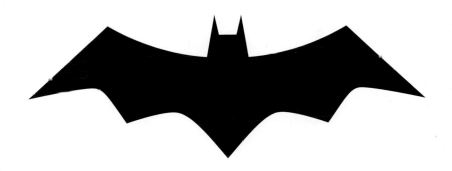

Knock, knock!
Who's there?
Wayne
Wayne who?
**Wayne the bathtub,
I'm dwowning!**

Knock, knock!

Who's there?

Police

Police who?

Po-lice open the door!
It's the Gotham City police!

Knock, knock!

Who's there?

Kook

Kook who?

**Don't call me cuckoo!
The name's the Joker!**

Knock, knock!

Who's there?

Ken.

Ken who?

**Ken I come in? The Joker's
on the loose!**

Knock, knock!

Who's there?

Alex.

Alex who?

Alex plain on the way to the Batcave, Robin!

Knock, knock!
Who's there?
Sparrow
Sparrow who?
Sparrow me all the questions, this is Robin, Boy Wonder!

Knock, knock!
Who's there?
Wanda
Wanda who?
Wanda go hang out with Robin?

Knock, knock!
Who's there?
Justin
Justin who?
Justin the Batcave for the very first time!

Knock, knock!
Who's there?
Raven
Raven who?
Raven lunatic, the Penguin! Quack, quack!

Knock, knock!
Who's there?
Tank.
Tank who?
Tank who for saving me, Batman!

Knock, knock!
Who's there?
Doris
Doris who?
Doris locked, so Batman will break it down!

Knock, knock!
Who's there?
Wayne.
Wayne who?
**Wayne drops keep
falling on my head!**

Knock, knock!
Who's there?
Bruce.
Bruce who?
**Bruce some
coffee for us,
I'm coming in!**

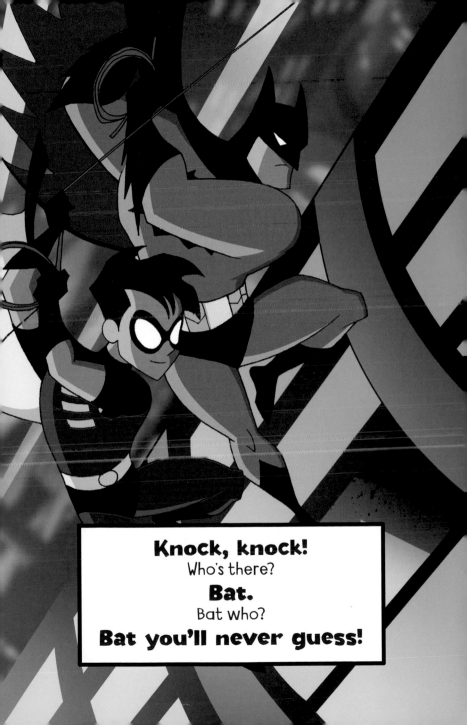

Knock, knock!
Who's there?
Irish
Irish who?
Irish I was Green Lantern!

Knock, knock!
Who's there?
Lantern
Lantern who?

Lantern down
on the runway!

Knock, knock!
Who's there?
Tess
Tess who?
**Tess out this new aircraft,
Hal Jordan!**

Knock, knock!
Who's there?
Gus
Gus who?

Gus he has a cool power ring, that's why!

THE FLASH!

Knock, knock!
Who's there?
Kenny
Kenny who?
Kenny outrun The Flash?

Knock, knock!

Who's there?

The Flash

The Flash who?

The Flash doesn't have a last name. It's just The Flash!

Knock, knock!

Who's there?

Barry.

Barry who?

Barry the treasure where no one will find it!

AQUAMAN!

Knock, knock!
Who's there?
Howard
Howard who?
**Howard you like to
go swimming with
Aquaman?**

Knock, knock!
Who's there?
Philip
Philip who?
**Philip this glass because
Aqualad is thirsty!**

Knock, knock!
Who's there?
Manta
Manta who?
**What's the Manta
with you?**

AND MORE!

Knock knock.

Who's there?

Interrupting Hawkman.

Interrupting Haw—

SKRREEEEE!

Knock knock.

Who's there?

Interrupting Joker.

Interrupting Jok—

HAHAHAHA!

Knock, knock!
Who's there?
Bumblebee
Bumblebee who?
Bumblebee nice and open the door!

Knock, knock!
Who's there?
Hawk
Hawk who?
Hawk come you won't open the door?

Knock, knock!

Who's there?

Martian

Martian who?

Martian in the super hero parade!

Knock, knock!
Who's there?
Atom
Atom who?
Atom all up, this is the tenth time I've knocked!

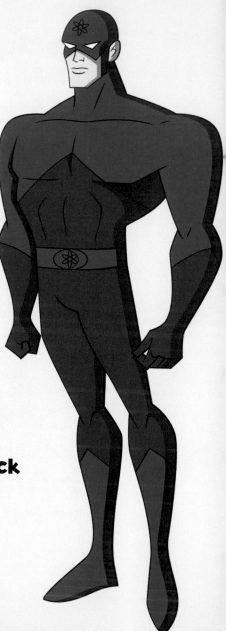

Knock, knock!
Who's there?
Ben
Ben who?
Ben down and pick me up, it's the Atom!

HOW TO TELL JOKES!

1. KNOW the joke.

Make sure you remember the whole joke before you tell it. This sounds like a no-brainer, but most of us have known someone who says, "Oh, this is so funny . . ." Then, when they tell the joke, they can't remember the end. And that's the whole point of a joke — its punch line.

2. SPEAK CLEARLY.

Don't mumble; don't speak too fast or too slow. Just speak like you normally do. You don't have to use a different voice or accent or sound like someone else.

3. LOOK at your audience.

Good eye contact with your listeners will grab their attention.

4. DON'T WORRY about gestures or how to stand or sit when you tell your joke. Remember, telling a joke is basically talking.

5. DON'T LAUGH at your own joke.

Yeah, yeah, I know some comedians break up while they're acting in a sketch or telling a story, but the best rule to follow is not to laugh. If you start to laugh, you might lose the rhythm of your joke or keep yourself from telling the joke clearly. Let your audience laugh. That's their job. Your job is to be the funny one.

6. THE PUNCH LINE is the most important part of the joke.

It's the climax, the payoff, the main event. A good joke can sound even better if you pause for just a second or two before you deliver the punch line. That tiny pause will make your audience mentally sit up and hold their breath, eager to hear what's coming next.

7. The SETUP is the second most important part of a joke.

That's basically everything you say before you get to the punch line. And that's why you need to be as clear as you can (see 2) so that when you finally reach the punch line, it makes sense!

8. YOU CAN GET FUNNIER.

It's easy. Watch other comedians. Listen to other people tell a joke or story. Check out a good comedy show or film. You can pick up some skills simply by seeing how others get their comedy across. You will absorb it! And soon it will come naturally.

9. Last, but not least, telling a joke is all about TIMING.

That means not only getting the biggest impact for your joke, waiting for the right time, giving that extra pause before the punch line — but it also means knowing when NOT to tell a joke. When you're among friends, you can tell when they'd like to hear something funny. But in an unfamiliar setting, get a "sense of the room" first. Are people having a good time? Or is it a more serious event? A joke has the most funny power when it's told in the right setting.

MICHAEL DAHL

Michael Dahl is the prolific author of the bestselling *Goodnight, Baseball* picture book and more than 200 other books for children and young adults. He has won the AEP Distinguished Achievement Award three times for his nonfiction, a Teacher's Choice award from *Learning* magazine, and a Seal of Excellence from the Creative Child Awards. And he has won awards for his board books for the earliest learners, *Duck Goes Potty* and *Bear Says "Thank You!"* Dahl has written and edited numerous graphic novels for younger readers, authored the Library of Doom adventure series, the Dragonblood books, Trollhunters, and the Hocus Pocus Hotel mystery/comedy series. Dahl has spoken at schools, libraries, and conferences across the US and the UK, including ALA, AASL, IRA, and Renaissance Learning. He currently lives in Minneapolis, Minnesota in a haunted house.

DONALD LEMKE

Donald Lemke works as a children's book editor. He has written dozens of all-age comics and children's books for Capstone, HarperCollins, Running Press, and more. Donald lives in St. Paul, Minnesota with his brilliant wife, Amy, two toddling toddlers, and a not-so-golden retriever named Paulie.

JOKE DICTIONARY!

bit (BIT)—a section of a comedy routine

comedian (kuh-MEE-dee-uhn)—an entertainer who makes people laugh

headliner (HED-lye-ner)—the last comedian to perform in a show

improvisation (im-PRAH-vuh-ZAY-shuhn)—a performance that hasn't been planned: "improv" for short

lineup (LINE-uhp)—a list of people who are going to perform in a show

one-liner (WUHN-lye-ner)—a short joke or funny remark

open mike (OH-puhn MIKE)—an event at which anyone can use the microphone to perform for the audience

punch line (PUHNCH line)—the words at the end of a joke that make it funny or surprising

shtick (SHTIK)—a repetitive, comic performance or routine

segue (SEG-way)—a sentence or phrase that leads from one joke or routine to another

stand-up (STAND-uhp)—the type of comedy performed while standing alone on stage

timing (TIME-ing)—the use of rhythm and tempo to make a joke funnier

HA!

HA!

HA!

DC SUPER HEROES

JOKE BOOKS

HA!

HA!

HA!

Only from...
**STONE ARCH
BOOKS!**

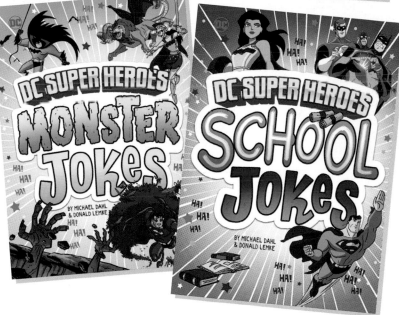